CW00860010

Entertainment Directory

CALGARY
RESTAURANT
GUIDE 2017

RESTAURANTS, BARS & CAFES

☆☆☆☆☆

The Most Positively
Reviewed and Recommended
Restaurants in the City

ECP
Editorial

CALGARY RESTAURANT GUIDE 2017
Best Rated Restaurants in Calgary, Canada

© Michael B. Déry, 2017
© E.G.P. Editorial, 2017

Printed in USA.

ISBN-13: 978-1537572628
ISBN-10: 1537572628

CALGARY RESTAURANTS 2017

The Most Recommended Restaurants in Calgary

This directory is dedicated to Calgary Business Owners and Managers who provide the experience that the locals and tourists enjoy. Thanks you very much for all that you do and thank for being the "People Choice".

Thanks to everyone that posts their reviews online and the amazing reviews sites that make our life easier.

The places listed in this book are the most positively reviewed and recommended by locals and travelers from around the world.

Thank you for your time and enjoy the directory that is designed with locals and tourist in mind!

TOP 500
RESTAURANTS
Ranked from #1 to #500

#1
Rosso Coffee Roasters
Cuisines: Coffee, Tea, Breakfast & Brunch
Average Price: Modest
Address: 803 24th Avenue SE
Calgary, AB T2G 4G5
Phone: (403) 971-1800

#2
Vendome Café
Cuisines: Breakfast & Brunch, Coffee, Tea
Average Price: Modest
Address: 940 2nd Avenue NW
Calgary, AB T2N 0E6
Phone: (403) 453-1140

#3
Lina's Italian Market
Cuisines: Caterer, Deli, Grocery, Coffee, Tea
Average Price: Modest
Address: 2202 Centre St NE
Calgary, AB T2E 2T5
Phone: (403) 277-9166

#4
Peppino
Cuisines: Italian, Ice Cream, Caterer
Average Price: Inexpensive
Address: 1240 Kensington Rd NW
Calgary, AB T2N 3P7
Phone: (403) 283-5350

#5
Beer Revolution
Cuisines: Pizza, Brewerie
Average Price: Modest
Address: 1080 8 Street SW
Calgary, AB T2R 0J3
Phone: (403) 264-2739

#6
Analog Coffee 17th Ave
Cuisines: Café, Coffee, Tea
Average Price: Inexpensive
Address: 740 17th Avenue SW
Calgary, AB T2T 0E7
Phone: (403) 265-2112

#7
Edelweiss Village
Cuisines: Deli, Sandwiches, Ethnic Food
Average Price: Modest
Address: 1921 20 Ave NW
Calgary, AB T2M 1H6
Phone: (403) 282-6600

#8
The Lazy Loaf & Kettle
Cuisines: Breakfast & Brunch, Bakery, Sandwiches
Average Price: Modest
Address: 8 Parkdale Crescent NW
Calgary, AB T2N 3T8
Phone: (403) 270-7810

#9
Sidewalk Citizen Bakery
Cuisines: Bakery, Sandwiches
Average Price: Modest
Address: 338 10 Street NW
Calgary, AB T2N 1V8
Phone: (403) 460-9065

#10
Rustic Sourdough Bakery
Cuisines: Deli, Sandwiches, Bakery
Average Price: Modest
Address: 1305 17 Avenue SW
Calgary, AB T2T 0C4
Phone: (403) 245-2113

#11
One Way Foods
Cuisines: Grocery, Deli
Average Price: Inexpensive
Address: 1740 11 Avenue SW
Calgary, AB T3C 0N4
Phone: (403) 245-3111

#12
Big Catch
Cuisines: Farmers Market, Japanese, Sushi Bar
Average Price: Modest
Address: 7711 Macleod Trail S
Calgary, AB T2H 0M1
Phone: (403) 708-5555

#13
European Bakery & Deli
Cuisines: Bakery, Deli
Average Price: Inexpensive
Address: 515 17 Avenue SW
Calgary, AB T2S 0A9
Phone: (403) 806-3768

#14
Brava Bistro
Cuisines: French, Beer, Wine, Spirits
Average Price: Expensive
Address: 723 17 Avenue SW
Calgary, AB T2S 0B6
Phone: (403) 228-1854

#15
Jojo's BBQ
Cuisines: Barbeque, Street Vendor
Average Price: Modest
Address: 3505 Edmonton Trl NE
Calgary, AB T2E 2H8
Phone: (587) 896-7827

#16
Wild Rose Brewery
Cuisines: Brewerie
Average Price: Modest
Address: 4580 Quesnay Wood Drive SW
Calgary, AB T3E 7J3
Phone: (403) 720-2733

#17
Creteus
Cuisines: Greek, Ethnic Food
Average Price: Inexpensive
Address: 17 Avenue SW
Calgary, AB T3E 0A5
Phone: (403) 246-4777

#18
Itea Bubble Tea And Coffee
Cuisines: Taiwanese, Coffee, Tea
Average Price: Inexpensive
Address: 312 Centre Street S
Calgary, AB T2G 2B8
Phone: (403) 999-9801

#19
The Italian Store
Cuisines: Deli, Sandwiches, Grocery
Average Price: Modest
Address: 5140 Skyline Way NE
Calgary, AB T2E 6V1
Phone: (403) 275-3300

#20
Bangkoknoi Thai Restaurant
Cuisines: Thai, Specialty Food
Average Price: Modest
Address: 1324 D Centre Street NE
Calgary, AB T2E 2R7
Phone: (403) 277-8424

#21
Bite Groceteria
Cuisines: Grocery, Deli, Ice Cream
Average Price: Modest
Address: 1023 9th Avenue SE
Calgary, AB T2G 0T1
Phone: (403) 263-3966

#22
Billingsgate Seafood Market
Cuisines: Seafood Market, Seafood
Average Price: Modest
Address: 1941 Uxbridge Drive NW
Calgary, AB T2N 2V2
Phone: (403) 269-3474

#23
Salsita
Cuisines: Ethnic Food, Grocery, Mexican
Average Price: Modest
Address: 777 Northmount Dr NW
Calgary, AB T2L 0A1
Phone: (403) 289-2202

#24
Rosso Coffee Roasters
Cuisines: Coffee, Tea, Breakfast & Brunch
Average Price: Inexpensive
Address: 425 11 Avenue SE
Calgary, AB T2G 0Y4
Phone: (587) 352-5080

#25
Sunterra Market, Britannia Plaza
Cuisines: Deli, Meat Shop, Grocery
Average Price: Expensive
Address: 803 49 Avenue SW
Calgary, AB T2S 1G8
Phone: (403) 287-0553

#26
Freak Lunchbox
Cuisines: Candy Store
Average Price: Inexpensive
Address: 614A 17th Avenue SW
Calgary, AB T2S 0B3
Phone: (403) 228-4480

#27
Shawarma And Falafel City
Cuisines: Falafel, Donairs
Average Price: Inexpensive
Address: 1245 Kensington Road NW
Calgary, AB T2N 3P7
Phone: (403) 452-4979

#28
Insadong Korean BBQ Restaurant
Cuisines: Ethnic Food, Korean, Barbeque
Average Price: Modest
Address: 132 920 36th Street NE
Calgary, AB T2A 6L8
Phone: (587) 353-3273

#29
Jerusalem Shawarma & Bakery
Cuisines: Donairs, Mediterranean, Arabian
Average Price: Modest
Address: 30 Country Hills Landing NW
Calgary, AB T3K 5P4
Phone: (403) 400-0341

#30
The Bake Chef Company
Cuisines: Bakery, Vietnamese
Average Price: Inexpensive
Address: 2500 University Drive NW
Calgary, AB T2N 1N4
Phone: (403) 282-6652

#31
Illichmann's Sausage Shop
Cuisines: Deli, Meat Shop, Sandwiches
Average Price: Modest
Address: 1840 36 St SE
Calgary, AB T2B 0X6
Phone: (403) 272-1673

#33
The Silk Road Spice Merchant
Cuisines: Specialty Food
Average Price: Modest
Address: 1403A - 9th Avenue SE
Calgary, AB T2G 0T4
Phone: (403) 261-1955

#32
Yann Haute Patisserie
Cuisines: Bakery, Desserts, Specialty Food
Average Price: Modest
Address: 329 23rd Avenue SW
Calgary, AB T2S 0J3
Phone: (403) 244-8091

#34
La Boulangerie
Cuisines: Bakery
Average Price: Modest
Address: 2435 4th Street SW
Calgary, AB T2S 1X2
Phone: (403) 984-9294

#35
Joycee's Caribbean Food & Takeout
Cuisines: Caribbean, Meat Shop
Average Price: Modest
Address: 630 1 Ave NE
Calgary, AB T2E 0B6
Phone: (403) 234-9940

#36
Dragon Gate Restaurant
Cuisines: Chinese, Ethnic Food
Average Price: Modest
Address: 2024 33 Ave SW
Calgary, AB T2T 1Z4
Phone: (403) 242-2210

#37
Golden Inn Restaurant
Cuisines: Caterer, Chinese, Ethnic Food
Average Price: Modest
Address: 107A 2nd Ave SE
Calgary, AB T2G 0B2
Phone: (403) 269-2211

#38
Brûlée Bakery
Cuisines: Bakery, Desserts
Average Price: Modest
Address: 722 11 Ave SW
Calgary, AB T2R 0E4
Phone: (403) 261-3064

#39
Kalamata Grocery Store
Cuisines: Grocery
Average Price: Modest
Address: 1421 11 Street SW
Calgary, AB T2R 1G7
Phone: (403) 244-0220

#40
**Manuel Latruwe Belgian
Patisserie & Bread Shop**
Cuisines: Bakery, Desserts
Average Price: Expensive
Address: 1333 1 Street SE
Calgary, AB T2G 5L1
Phone: (403) 261-1092

#41
Crave Cookies And Cupcakes
Cuisines: Bakery, Desserts, Gluten-Free
Average Price: Expensive
Address: 318 Aspen Glen Landing SW
Calgary, AB T3H 0N5
Phone: (403) 221-8307

#42
Pop's Dairy Bar
Cuisines: Ice Cream, Hot Dogs, Desserts
Average Price: Modest
Address: 1024 Bellevue Ave SE
Calgary, AB T2G 4L1
Phone: (403) 452-4310

#43
Pâtisserie Du Soleil
Cuisines: Bakery, Desserts,
Breakfast & Brunch
Average Price: Modest
Address: 2525 Woodview Drive SW
Calgary, AB T2W 4N4
Phone: (403) 452-8833

#44
**Polcan Meat Products
& Delicatessen**
Cuisines: Deli, Sandwiches, Meat Shop
Average Price: Modest
Address: 357 Heritage Dr SE
Calgary, AB T2H 1M8
Phone: (403) 258-0228

#45
Canvas Coffee & Wine
Cuisines: Coffee, Tea,
Breakfast & Brunch, Tapas
Average Price: Modest
Address: 602 11th Avenue SW
Calgary, AB T2R 1J8
Phone: (587) 353-1299

#46
European Delicatessen & Bakery
Cuisines: Deli, Sandwiches, Meat Shop
Average Price: Inexpensive
Address: 8409 Elbow Drive SW
Calgary, AB T2V 1K8
Phone: (403) 244-0570

#47
Willow Park Wines & Spirits
Cuisines: Beer, Wine, Spirits
Average Price: Modest
Address: 10801 Bonaventure Dr SE
Calgary, AB T2J 6Z8
Phone: (403) 296-1640

#48
Dell Cafe
Cuisines: Sandwiches, Coffee, Tea, Burgers
Average Price: Inexpensive
Address: 7930 Bowness Road NW
Calgary, AB T3B 0H3
Phone: (403) 288-3606

#49
Bumpy's Cafe
Cuisines: Coffee, Tea
Average Price: Modest
Address: 1040 8 Street SW
Calgary, AB T2R 1K2
Phone: (403) 265-0244

#50
Great Canadian Bagel
Cuisines: Bagels, Deli
Average Price: Inexpensive
Address: 311-17 Avenue SW
Calgary, AB T2S 0A3
Phone: (403) 209-2022

#51
Calgary Meats & Deli
Cuisines: Deli, Sandwiches, Meat Shop
Average Price: Modest
Address: 1204 Edmonton Trl NE
Calgary, AB T2E 3K5
Phone: (403) 276-1423

#52
Market 17
Cuisines: Grocery, Organic Store,
Health Market
Average Price: Modest
Address: 17 Avenue & 24th Street SW
Calgary, AB T3C 1J2
Phone: (403) 685-4410

#53
Gummi Boutique
Cuisines: Candy Store
Average Price: Inexpensive
Address: 205 10th Street NW
Calgary, AB T2N 1V5
Phone: (587) 353-0031

#54
Lloyd's Patty Plus
Cuisines: Bakery, Caribbean
Average Price: Inexpensive
Address: 255 28 Street SE
Calgary, AB T2A 5K4
Phone: (403) 207-4455

#55
Big Star Bakehouse
Cuisines: Bakery, Gluten-Free
Average Price: Expensive
Address: 1510 6 St SW
Calgary, AB T2R 0R7
Phone: (403) 452-6572

#56
Waves Coffee House
Cuisines: Venues, Event Space,
Coffee, Tea, Café
Average Price: Inexpensive
Address: 2685 36 St. NE
Calgary, AB T1Y 5S3
Phone: (587) 350-8838

#57
Pharaoh's
Cuisines: Middle Eastern, Food
Average Price: Inexpensive
Address: 1610 10 St SW
Calgary, AB T2R 1G1
Phone: (403) 888-6000

#58
Postino Cafe & Lounge
Cuisines: Coffee, Tea, Lounge, Café
Average Price: Inexpensive
Address: 2502 Capital Hill Crescent NW
Calgary, AB T2M 4C2
Phone: (403) 338-0633

#59
Deville Luxury Coffee & Pastries
Cuisines: Coffee, Tea, Internet Café
Average Price: Modest
Address: 807 1st Street SW
Calgary, AB T2P 7N2
Phone: (403) 263-0884

#60
The Mongolie Grill
Cuisines: Mongolian, Ethnic Food
Average Price: Modest
Address: 1108 4 St SW
Calgary, AB T2R 0X6
Phone: (403) 262-7773

#61
Lazy Monkey
Cuisines: Café, Taiwanese, Coffee, Tea
Average Price: Modest
Address: 3616 52nd Avenue NW
Calgary, AB T2L 1V9
Phone: (403) 338-2123

#62
Crossroads Market
Cuisines: Farmers Market, Grocery
Average Price: Inexpensive
Address: 1235 26 Avenue SE
Calgary, AB T2G 1R7
Phone: (403) 291-5208

#63
Calgary Co-Op
Cuisines: Grocery
Average Price: Modest
Address: 1130 11 Avenue SW
Calgary, AB T2R 0G4
Phone: (403) 299-4257

#64
La Tiendona Market
Cuisines: Grocery
Average Price: Modest
Address: 1836 36 St SE
Calgary, AB T2B 0X6
Phone: (403) 272-4054

#65
Jelly Modern Doughnuts
Cuisines: Donuts
Average Price: Modest
Address: 1414 8 St SW
Calgary, AB T2R 1J6
Phone: (403) 453-2053

#66
Oolong Tea House
Cuisines: Coffee, Tea
Average Price: Inexpensive
Address: 110 10 Street NW
Calgary, AB T2N 1V3
Phone: (403) 283-0333

#67
Montreal Bagels
Cuisines: Bagels
Average Price: Inexpensive
Address: 8408 Elbow Drive SW
Calgary, AB T2V 1K7
Phone: (403) 212-4060

#68
DavidsTea
Cuisines: Coffee, Tea, Tea Room
Average Price: Modest
Address: 203 8 Avenue SW
Calgary, AB T2P 1B5
Phone: (403) 264-0325

#69
Decadent Desserts
Cuisines: Bakery, Desserts
Average Price: Expensive
Address: 831 10 Ave SW
Calgary, AB T2R 0B4
Phone: (403) 282-3392

#70
The Coffee Couch
Cuisines: Coffee, Tea, Café
Average Price: Modest
Address: 128 28 Street SE
Calgary, AB T2A 6J9
Phone: (403) 235-6884

#71
Sunterra Market- Keynote
Cuisines: Grocery
Average Price: Modest
Address: 200 12 Avenue SE
Calgary, AB T2G 0Z7
Phone: (403) 261-6772

#72
Choklat
Cuisines: Chocolate Shop
Average Price: Modest
Address: 1327A 9th Avenue SE
Calgary, AB T2G 0T2
Phone: (403) 457-1419

#73
Les chocolats de Chloé
Cuisines: Chocolate Shop
Average Price: Modest
Address: 375 Rue Roy E
Montreal, QC H2W 1N1
Phone: (514) 849-5550

#74
Avenue Deli
Cuisines: Coffee, Tea, Deli
Average Price: Modest
Address: 2008 33 Ave SW
Calgary, AB T2T 1Z4
Phone: (403) 242-6783

#75
Safeway Food & Drug
Cuisines: Deli, Grocery
Average Price: Modest
Address: 813 11 Avenue SW
Calgary, AB T2R 0E6
Phone: (403) 266-5640

#76
Delightful Cafe
Cuisines: Coffee, Tea, Vietnamese,
Breakfast & Brunch
Average Price: Inexpensive
Address: 1201 9th Avenue SE
Calgary, AB T2G 0S9
Phone: (403) 262-2220

#77
Sidewalk Citizen Bakery
Cuisines: Bakery
Average Price: Inexpensive
Address: 2, 5524 1A Street SW
Calgary, AB T2H
Phone: (403) 457-2245

#78
Sunny's Hamburger
Cuisines: Food, Burgers
Average Price: Inexpensive
Address: 7003 Ogden Road
Calgary, AB T2C 1B4
Phone: (403) 279-3802

#79
Maria Market
Cuisines: Deli, Grocery
Average Price: Inexpensive
Address: 2770 32nd Ave NE
Calgary, AB T1Y 5S5
Phone: (403) 291-6828

#80
Try Again Beverage's House
Cuisines: Coffee, Tea
Average Price: Inexpensive
Address: 111 3 Avenue SE
Calgary, AB T2G 4Z4
Phone: (403) 234-0666

#81
Italian Supermarket
Cuisines: Grocery
Average Price: Modest
Address: 265 20 Avenue NE
Calgary, AB T2E 1R1
Phone: (403) 277-7875

#82
Fratello Analog Cafe
Cuisines: Coffee, Tea
Average Price: Modest
Address: Calgary Farmer's Market
Calgary, AB T2H 1C3
Phone: (403) 265-2112

#83
Higher Ground
Cuisines: Coffee, Tea, Internet Café
Average Price: Modest
Address: 1126 Kensington Road NW
Calgary, AB T2N 3P3
Phone: (403) 270-3780

#84
Dairy Queen
Cuisines: Fast Food, Ice Cream
Average Price: Inexpensive
Address: 1403 8 Street SW
Calgary, AB T2R 1B8
Phone: (403) 229-2909

#85
Glamorgan Bakery
Cuisines: Bakery
Average Price: Inexpensive
Address: 3919 Richmond Road SW
Calgary, AB T3E 4P2
Phone: (403) 242-2800

#86
ATCO Blue Flame Kitchen Cafe
Cuisines: Café, Coffee, Tea
Average Price: Modest
Address: 911 11 Avenue SW
Calgary, AB T2R 0E7
Phone: (403) 460-7546

#87
Village Pita Bakery
Cuisines: Bakery
Average Price: Inexpensive
Address: 255 28 St SE
Calgary, AB T2A 5K4
Phone: (403) 273-0330

#88
Unimarket
Cuisines: Ethnic Food, Mexican, Grocery
Average Price: Modest
Address: 128 50th Avenue SE
Calgary, AB T2G 5N3
Phone: (403) 255-4479

#89
Shef's Fiery Kitchen
Cuisines: Thai, Farmers Market,
Indian, Cooking School
Average Price: Inexpensive
Address: 510 77 Avenue SE
Calgary, AB T2H 1C3
Phone: (403) 918-7433

#90
Cornerstone Music Cafe'
Cuisines: Café, Coffee, Tea
Average Price: Modest
Address: 14919 Deer Ridge Drive SE
Calgary, AB T2J 7C4
Phone: (403) 278-3070

#91
The Naked Leaf
Cuisines: Coffee, Tea
Average Price: Expensive
Address: #4 - 1126 Kensington Rd. NW
Calgary, AB T2N 3P3
Phone: (403) 283-3555

#92
Bagelino's The Bagel Company
Cuisines: Bagels, Sandwiches
Average Price: Inexpensive
Address: 809 7 Street SW
Calgary, AB T2P 1Z5
Phone: (403) 265-2118

#93
Waves Coffee House
Cuisines: Coffee, Tea
Average Price: Modest
Address: 1019 17th Avenue SW
Calgary, AB T2T 0A7
Phone: (403) 457-5441

#94
Vagabond Brewery And Restaurant
Cuisines: Canadian, Brewerie
Average Price: Modest
Address: 1129 Olympic Way SE
Calgary, AB T2G 0L4
Phone: (403) 474-0699

#95
**Atlas Specialty Supermarket
& Persian Cuisine**
Cuisines: Middle Eastern,
Grocery, Persian, Iranian
Average Price: Modest
Address: 1000 9 Ave SW
Calgary, AB T2P 2Y6
Phone: (403) 230-0990

#96
Signature Palace Restaurant
Cuisines: Ethnic Food, Chinese
Average Price: Modest
Address: 1919 Sirocco Drive SW
Calgary, AB T3H 2Y3
Phone: (403) 246-8883

#97
Lindt Outlet Boutique
Cuisines: Chocolate Shop
Average Price: Modest
Address: 4th Street SW
Calgary, AB T2R 0Y2
Phone: (403) 802-1171

#98
Shanghai Fine Food
Cuisines: Street Vendor
Average Price: Modest
Address: 510 77th Ave SE
Calgary, AB T2H 1C3
Phone: (403) 240-9113

#99
Franca's
Cuisines: Coffee, Tea, Italian
Average Price: Modest
Address: 3811 Edmonton Trail NE
Calgary, AB T2E 3P5
Phone: (403) 277-0766

#100
Holy Smoke BBQ
Cuisines: Specialty Food, Barbeque
Average Price: Modest
Address: 901 64 Avenue NE
Calgary, AB T2E 9B7
Phone: (403) 264-1185

#101
Vine Arts
Cuisines: Beer, Wine, Spirits
Average Price: Modest
Address: 1310 1st St SW
Calgary, AB T2R 0V7
Phone: (403) 290-0700

#102
Redheads Bagel Cafe
Cuisines: Bagels, Café
Average Price: Modest
Address: 638 11th Ave SW
Calgary, AB T2R 0E2
Phone: (403) 532-0600

#103
Calgary Farmers Market
Cuisines: Farmers Market
Average Price: Modest
Address: 510 77th Avenue SE
Calgary, AB T2H 1C3
Phone: (403) 240-9113

#104
Luxor Emporium Cafe
Cuisines: Middle Eastern, Ethnic Food
Average Price: Modest
Address: 937 7 Avenue SW
Calgary, AB T2P 1A5
Phone: (403) 282-0030

#105
Melly's Bakery & Cafe
Cuisines: Bakery
Average Price: Inexpensive
Address: 112- 6800 Memorial Dr NE
Calgary, AB T2A 6V3
Phone: (403) 569-1517

#106
Sunterra Market,
West Market Square
Cuisines: Meat Shop, Grocery
Average Price: Expensive
Address: 1851 Sirocco Drive SW
Calgary, AB T3H 4R5
Phone: (403) 266-3049

#107
Cookie Mama
Cuisines: Desserts
Average Price: Modest
Address: 1420 9 Ave SE
Calgary, AB T2G 0T5
Phone: (403) 266-5431

#108
Humpty's Diner
Cuisines: Desserts, Diner
Average Price: Modest
Address: 7007 11 St SE
Calgary, AB T2H 2T9
Phone: (403) 252-3067

#109
Tutti Frutti
Cuisines: Ice Cream
Average Price: Inexpensive
Address: 858 16 Avenue SW
Calgary, AB T2R 0S9
Phone: (403) 460-8846

#110
Gummi Boutique
Cuisines: Candy Store, Toy Store
Average Price: Modest
Address: 3919 Richmond Rd SW
Calgary, AB T3E 4P2
Phone: (403) 457-4864

#111
Safeway Food & Drug
Cuisines: Deli, Sandwiches, Grocery
Average Price: Modest
Address: 9737 Macleod Trl SW
Calgary, AB T2J 0P6
Phone: (403) 252-8123

#112
Tim Hortons
Cuisines: Coffee, Tea, Donuts, Sandwiches
Average Price: Inexpensive
Address: 11488 24 St SE
Calgary, AB T2Z 4C9
Phone: (403) 236-3749

#113
Fiasco Gelato
Cuisines: Ice Cream, Street Vendor, Desserts
Average Price: Inexpensive
Address: 416 Meridian Road SE
Calgary, AB T2A 1X2
Phone: (403) 452-3150

#114
Crave Cookies & Cupcakes
Cuisines: Bakery, Desserts
Average Price: Modest
Address: 10816 Macleod Trail SE,
Suite 222 Calgary, AB T2J
Phone: (403) 270-2728

#115
Byblos Bakery Ltd
Cuisines: Bakery
Average Price: Inexpensive
Address: 2479 23 Street NE
Calgary, AB T2E 8J8
Phone: (403) 250-3711

#116
The Buttercream Bake Shoppe
Cuisines: Desserts, Bakery
Average Price: Expensive
Address: 121 - 1013 17th Ave SW
Calgary, AB T2T 0A7
Phone: (403) 228-9900

#117
Menchie's
Cuisines: Ice Cream
Average Price: Modest
Address: 4820 Northland Drive NW
Calgary, AB T2L 2L3
Phone: (403) 460-7871

#118
The Light Cellar
Cuisines: Grocery
Average Price: Modest
Address: 6326 Bowness Road NW
Calgary, AB T3B 0E5
Phone: (403) 453-1343

#119
Highlander Wine & Spirits
Cuisines: Beer, Wine, Spirits
Average Price: Modest
Address: 2033 16 Avenue NW
Calgary, AB T2M 0M3
Phone: (403) 282-2442

#120
The House Coffee & Sanctuary
Cuisines: Coffee, Tea
Average Price: Modest
Address: 126 10 Street NW
Calgary, AB T2N 1V3
Phone: (403) 283-7879

#121
Lukes Drug Mart
Cuisines: Drugstore, Coffee, Tea
Average Price: Modest
Address: 112 4th Street NE
Calgary, AB T2E 3R9
Phone: (403) 266-4142

#122
Rosso Coffee Roasters
Cuisines: Coffee, Tea, Breakfast & Brunch
Average Price: Modest
Address: 140 8th Avenue SE
Calgary, AB T2G 0K6
Phone: (403) 264-7900

#123
Janice Beaton Fine Cheese
Cuisines: Cheese Shop
Average Price: Expensive
Address: 1017 16th Ave SW
Calgary, AB T2R 0T5
Phone: (403) 806-0500

#124
Kawa Espresso Bar
Cuisines: Coffee, Tea
Average Price: Modest
Address: 1333 8 Street SW
Calgary, AB T2P
Phone: (403) 452-5233

#125
Los Compadres
Cuisines: Mexican, Food Truck, Fast Food
Average Price: Modest
Address: 1439 17th Avenue SW
Calgary, AB T2T
Phone: (403) 460-2770

#126
Tea Funny
Cuisines: Coffee, Tea
Average Price: Modest
Address: 123 - 1323 Centre St
Calgary, AB T2E 2R5
Phone: (403) 978-5888

#127
Euphoria Cafe
Cuisines: Juice Bar, Coffee, Tea, Ice Cream
Average Price: Modest
Address: 5403 Crowchild Trl NW
Calgary, AB T2N
Phone: (403) 313-0503

#128
The Better Butcher
Cuisines: Meat Shop, Butcher
Average Price: Modest
Address: 377 Heritage Drive SE
Calgary, AB T2H 1M8
Phone: (403) 252-7171

#129
The Tea Factory
Cuisines: Coffee, Tea, Tea Room
Average Price: Modest
Address: 1820 4th Street SW
Calgary, AB T2S 0C9
Phone: (403) 282-8828

#130
The Bean Stop
Cuisines: Coffee, Tea
Average Price: Modest
Address: 200 Barclay Parade SW
Calgary, AB T2P 4R5
Phone: (403) 261-0865

#131
Amato Gelato Cafe
Cuisines: Ice Cream
Average Price: Modest
Address: 2104 Kensington Road NW
Calgary, AB T2N 3R7
Phone: (403) 270-9733

#132
Springbank Cheese Company
Cuisines: Cheese Shop
Average Price: Modest
Address: 2015 14 St NW
Calgary, AB T2M 3N4
Phone: (403) 282-8331

#133
Second To None Meats
Cuisines: Meat Shop
Average Price: Modest
Address: 2100 4 Street SW
Calgary, AB T2S 1W7
Phone: (403) 245-6662

#134
Fresh Blend Coffee & Sandwich Bar
Cuisines: Coffee, Tea, Sandwiches
Average Price: Modest
Address: 4625 Varsity Drive NW
Calgary, AB T3A 0Z9
Phone: (403) 288-1888

#135
Tea Trader
Cuisines: Tea Room
Average Price: Modest
Address: 1228 A - 9 Ave SE
Calgary, AB T2G 0T1
Phone: (403) 264-0728

#136
My Favorite Ice Cream Shoppe
Cuisines: Ice Cream
Average Price: Inexpensive
Address: 2048 42 Ave SW
Calgary, AB T2T 2M7
Phone: (403) 287-3838

#137
Rocky's Sausage Haus
Cuisines: Butcher
Average Price: Modest
Address: 37 4th St NE
Calgary, AB T2E 3R7
Phone: (403) 266-2697

#138
Red Bush Tea And Coffee Company
Cuisines: Coffee, Tea
Average Price: Modest
Address: 225 10th Street NW
Calgary, AB T2N 1V5
Phone: (403) 270-7744

#139
Lund's Organics
Cuisines: Farmers Market
Average Price: Inexpensive
Address: 7711 Macleod Trail SW
Calgary, AB T2H 0M1
Phone: (403) 227-2693

#140
Epiphanie Chocolate
Cuisines: Chocolate Shop
Average Price: Expensive
Address: 1417B 11th Street SW
Calgary, AB T2R 1G5
Phone: (403) 370-4592

#141
Bell's Bookstore Cafe
Cuisines: Coffee, Tea, Bookstore
Average Price: Inexpensive
Address: 1515A 34 Ave SW
Calgary, AB T2T 2B1
Phone: (403) 243-3095

#142
Kensington Wine Market
Cuisines: Beer, Wine, Spirits
Average Price: Expensive
Address: 1257 Kensington Rd NW
Calgary, AB T2N 3P8
Phone: (403) 283-8000

#143
Metrovino
Cuisines: Beer, Wine, Spirits
Average Price: Modest
Address: 722 11 Ave SW
Calgary, AB T2R 0E4
Phone: (403) 205-3356

#144
Amandine Bakery
Cuisines: Bakery, Desserts
Average Price: Modest
Address: 2610 Centre Street. N
Calgary, AB T2E 2V4
Phone: (403) 276-3532

#145
Butcher And The Baker
Cuisines: Bakery, Sandwiches
Average Price: Modest
Address: 250 6th Avenue SW
Calgary, AB T2P 3H7
Phone: (403) 265-7765

#146
Starbucks
Cuisines: Coffee, Tea
Average Price: Inexpensive
Address: 2219 4th Street SW
Calgary, AB T2S 1X1
Phone: (403) 229-3008

#147
Oriental Dumplings
Cuisines: Chinese, Coffee, Tea, Juice Bar
Average Price: Inexpensive
Address: 1623 Center Street NW
Calgary, AB T2E 8S7
Phone: (403) 276-8816

#148
The Cookbook Co Cooks
Cuisines: Bookstore, Grocery,
Cooking School
Average Price: Expensive
Address: 722 11 Ave SW
Calgary, AB T2R 0E4
Phone: (403) 265-6066

#149
Leavitt's Ice Cream Shop
Cuisines: Ice Cream
Average Price: Modest
Address: 3410 3 Avenue NW
Calgary, AB T2N 0M2
Phone: (403) 283-3578

#150
Yamato Dessert Café
Cuisines: Desserts
Average Price: Modest
Address: 1322 Centre St NE
Calgary, AB T2E 2R7
Phone: (403) 230-5313

#151
Tim Hortons
Cuisines: Coffee, Tea, Fast Food,
Sandwiches
Average Price: Inexpensive
Address: 665 8 Street SW
Calgary, AB T2P 3E5
Phone: (403) 767-9957

#152
Good Earth Cafe
Cuisines: Coffee, Tea
Average Price: Modest
Address: 602 1st Street SW
Calgary, AB T2P
Phone: (403) 699-9610

#153
Wine Ink
Cuisines: Beer, Wine, Spirits
Average Price: Modest
Address: 932 17th Avenue SW
Calgary, AB T2T 0A2
Phone: (403) 229-1302

#154
Tim Hortons
Cuisines: Bakery, Coffee, Tea,
Donuts, Sandwiches
Average Price: Inexpensive
Address: 1103 17 Ave SW
Calgary, AB T2T 0B5
Phone: (403) 228-9899

#155
Davids Tea
Cuisines: Coffee, Tea, Tea Room
Average Price: Expensive
Address: 100 Anderson Road
Calgary, AB T2J 3V1
Phone: (403) 262-1548

#156
Peasant Cheese Shop
Cuisines: Cheese Shop, Caterer
Average Price: Modest
Address: 1249 Kensington Road NW
Calgary, AB T2N 3P7
Phone: (587) 353-3599

#157
Coppeneur Chocolate
Cuisines: Chocolate Shop
Average Price: Expensive
Address: 8th Avenue SW
Calgary, AB T2P 1B4
Phone: (403) 457-4210

#158
Prairie Mill Bread Company
Cuisines: Bakery
Average Price: Expensive
Address: 4820 Northland Dr NW
Calgary, AB T2L 2L4
Phone: (403) 282-6455

#159
The Purple Perk
Cuisines: Coffee, Tea
Average Price: Modest
Address: 2212 4 St SW
Calgary, AB T2S 1W9
Phone: (403) 244-1300

#160
Eclair De Lune
Cuisines: Bakery
Average Price: Modest
Address: 1049 40 Ave NW
Calgary, AB T2K 0G2
Phone: (403) 398-8803

#161
**Sunterra Market, Gulf
Canada Square**
Cuisines: Grocery
Average Price: Modest
Address: 401 9 Avenue SW
Calgary, AB T2P 3C5
Phone: (403) 263-9755

#162
Tutti Frutti Frozen Yogurt
Cuisines: Ice Cream
Average Price: Inexpensive
Address: 4307 130th Avenue SE
Calgary, AB T2Z 3V8
Phone: (403) 460-2481

#163
Wayne's Bagels
Cuisines: Bagels
Average Price: Inexpensive
Address: 4515 Macleod Trl SW
Calgary, AB T2G
Phone: (403) 270-7090

#164
Village Brewery
Cuisines: Brewerie
Average Price: Inexpensive
Address: 5000 12A St SE
Calgary, AB T2G 5L5
Phone: (403) 243-3327

#165
Roasterie
Cuisines: Coffee, Tea
Average Price: Inexpensive
Address: 314 10 St NW
Calgary, AB T2N 1V8
Phone: (403) 270-3304

#166
Enoteca
Cuisines: Beer, Wine, Spirits
Average Price: Expensive
Address: 7112 Macleod Trail SE
Calgary, AB T2H 0L3
Phone: (403) 252-5529

#167
**Pascal's Patisserie
Take & Bake French Pastries**
Cuisines: Bakery, Do-It-Yourself Food
Average Price: Expensive
Address: 5240 - 1A Street SE
Calgary, AB T2H 1J1
Phone: (403) 968-6156

#168
Bridgeland Market
Cuisines: Grocery
Average Price: Modest
Address: 1104 1 Avenue NE
Calgary, AB T2E 0C8
Phone: (403) 269-2381

#169
Little Monday Cafe
Cuisines: Café, Coffee, Tea
Average Price: Inexpensive
Address: 3401 Spruce Center SW
Calgary, AB T3C 0A5
Phone: (403) 454-5041

#170
ITZA Bakeshop
Cuisines: Bakery
Average Price: Expensive
Address: 111, 908 17 Ave. S.W.
Calgary, AB T2T 0A2
Phone: (403) 228-0044

#171
La Vida Loca Mexican
Restaurant & Fiesta Bar
Cuisines: Beer, Wine, Spirits, Mexican
Average Price: Modest
Address: 1129 17 Avenue SW
Calgary, AB T2T 0B4
Phone: (587) 349-1400

#172
Cobs Bread
Cuisines: Bakery
Average Price: Modest
Address: 7610 Elbow Dr SW
Calgary, AB T2V 1K2
Phone: (403) 253-2999

#173
Good Earth Cafes
Cuisines: Bakery, Coffee, Tea
Average Price: Modest
Address: 1502 11 St SW
Calgary, AB T2R 1G9
Phone: (403) 228-9543

#174
Chilis
Cuisines: Beer, Wine, Spirits, American
Average Price: Modest
Address: 2000 Airport Road NE
Calgary, AB T2E
Phone: (403) 291-4742

#175
Phil & Sebastian Coffee Roasters
Cuisines: Coffee, Tea
Average Price: Modest
Address: 2043 33rd Avenue SW
Calgary, AB T2T
Phone: (403) 686-1221

#176
Chuen May Food Products
Cuisines: Dim Sum, Ethnic Food
Average Price: Inexpensive
Address: 221 1 St SE
Calgary, AB T2G 2G3
Phone: (403) 232-8364

#177
Phil & Sebastian Coffee Roasters
Cuisines: Coffee, Tea
Average Price: Modest
Address: 2207 4 Street SW
Calgary, AB T2S 1W9
Phone: (403) 245-1111

#178
Mercato Foods
Cuisines: Grocery, Specialty Food
Average Price: Expensive
Address: 2224 4 St SW
Calgary, AB T2S 1W9
Phone: (403) 263-5535

#179
Starbucks
Cuisines: Coffee, Tea
Average Price: Modest
Address: 3531 Garrison Gate SW
Calgary, AB T2T 6E4
Phone: (403) 685-4500

#180
Edible Arrangements
Cuisines: Gift Shop, Florist, Chocolate Shop
Average Price: Modest
Address: 250 7th Ave SW
Calgary, AB T2P 0W6
Phone: (403) 269-3663

#181
Tutti Frutti
Cuisines: Desserts, Ice Cream
Average Price: Inexpensive
Address: 33 Heritage Meadows Way SE
Calgary, AB T2H 3B8
Phone: (403) 460-2987

#182
Gunther's Fine Baking
Cuisines: Bakery,
Average Price: Modest
Address: 4306 17 Avenue SE
Calgary, AB T2A 0T4
Phone: (403) 272-0383

#183
Calgary Co-op Liquor Store
Cuisines: Beer, Wine, Spirits
Average Price: Modest
Address: 5505 Shaganappi Trl NW
Calgary, AB T3A
Phone: (403) 299-4333

#184
Weeds Cafe
Cuisines: Coffee, Tea
Average Price: Modest
Address: 1903 20 Ave NW
Calgary, AB T2M 1H6
Phone: (403) 282-7940

#185
Korean Bakery
Cuisines: Bakery, Desserts
Average Price: Inexpensive
Address: #10 1324 10 Avenue SW
Calgary, AB T3C
Phone: (403) 802-2023

#186
Frogurt
Cuisines: Ice Cream
Average Price: Modest
Address: 1109b Kensington Road NW
Calgary, AB T2N 3P2
Phone: (403) 474-5600

#187
Aglio E Olio
Cuisines: Food Truck, Italian
Average Price: Modest
Address:
Calgary, AB
Phone: (403) 616-3560

#188
Chongo's Produce Market
Cuisines: Grocery, Farmers Market
Average Price: Modest
Address: 1235 26 Ave SE
Calgary, AB T2G 1R7
Phone: (403) 921-4554

#189
The Cellar
Cuisines: Beer, Wine, Spirits
Average Price: Expensive
Address: 137 8 Avenue SW
Calgary, AB T2P 1B4
Phone: (403) 503-0730

#190
Dairy Queen
Cuisines: Burgers, Ice Cream
Average Price: Inexpensive
Address: 8180 - 11th Street Southeast
Calgary, AB T2H 3B5
Phone: (403) 252-8230

#191
Real Canadian Wholesale Club
Cuisines: Grocery
Average Price: Inexpensive
Address: 222 58 Ave SE
Calgary, AB T2H 0N9
Phone: (403) 255-5590

#192
A Taste Of Quebec
Cuisines: Bakery, Deli
Average Price: Modest
Address: 510 77th Ave SE
Calgary, AB T2H 1C3
Phone: (403) 240-9113

#193
Canada Safeway Limited
Cuisines: Deli, Florist, Grocery
Average Price: Exclusive
Address: 1818 Centre Street NE
Calgary, AB T2E 2S6
Phone: (403) 276-3328

#194
Crowfoot Wine & Spirits
Cuisines: Beer, Wine, Spirits
Average Price: Modest
Address: 7414 Crowfoot Road NW
Calgary, AB T3G 3N7
Phone: (403) 296-2200

#195
The Bullet Cappuccino Bar
Cuisines: Coffee, Tea
Average Price: Modest
Address: 728 Northmount Dr NW
Calgary, AB T2K 3K2
Phone: (403) 244-1963

#196
Papa Chocolat
Cuisines: Chocolate Shop
Average Price: Exclusive
Address: 10816 Macleod Trail S
Calgary, AB T2J 5N8
Phone: (403) 264-7212

#197
Caribbean Choice Food
Cuisines: Caribbean, Grocery
Average Price: Modest
Address: 2235 Centre St NW
Calgary, AB T2E 2T4
Phone: (403) 230-1880

#198
Simple Simon Pies
Cuisines: Specialty Food
Average Price: Inexpensive
Address: 510 77th Ave SE
Calgary, AB T2H 1C3
Phone: (403) 205-3475

#199
SPUD
Cuisines: Grocery, Food Delivery Services
Average Price: Expensive
Address: 3200 14 Ave NE
Calgary, AB T2A 6J4
Phone: (403) 615-3663

#200
Petit Mousse
Cuisines: Farmers Market, French
Average Price: Inexpensive
Address: 77th Avenue SE
Calgary, AB T2H 1C3
Phone: (403) 668-1744

#201
Steakout Truck
Cuisines: Street Vendor, Food Truck
Average Price: Modest
Address: 827 10th Avenue SW
Calgary, AB T2R 0A9
Phone: (403) 261-9759

#202
Dairy Queen
Cuisines: Fast Food, Ice Cream
Average Price: Inexpensive
Address: 2126 Crowchild Trl NW
Calgary, AB T2M 3Y7
Phone: (403) 282-4947

#203
Purdy's Chocolates
Cuisines: Chocolate Shop, Ice Cream
Average Price: Modest
Address: 1632 14 Ave NW
Calgary, AB T2N 1M7
Phone: (403) 220-0334

#204
Good Earth Cafe
Cuisines: Café, Coffee, Tea
Average Price: Inexpensive
Address: 356 Cranston Road SE
Calgary, AB T3M 0S9
Phone: (403) 457-1997

#205
Bulk Barn
Cuisines: Grocery
Average Price: Modest
Address: 3508 32nd Avenue NE
Calgary, AB T1Y 6J2
Phone: (403) 250-1399

#206
Highlander Wine & Spirits
Cuisines: Beer, Wine, Spirits
Average Price: Modest
Address: 2919 Richmond Road SW
Calgary, AB T3E 4N3
Phone: (403) 233-2629

#207
The Nut Man Company
Cuisines: Specialty Food
Average Price: Modest
Address: 205 5 Ave SW
Calgary, AB T2P 2V7
Phone: (403) 266-4699

#208
Hoven Farms
Cuisines: Butcher
Average Price: Expensive
Address: 7711 Macleod Trail SW
Calgary, AB T2H 0M1
Phone: (403) 217-2343

#209
National Fine Food, Beer & Spirits
Cuisines: Canadian, Beer, Wine, Spirits
Average Price: Modest
Address: 180 Stewart Green SW
Calgary, AB T3H 3C8
Phone: (403) 685-6801

#210
Ten Ren's Tea Time
Cuisines: Taiwanese, Coffee, Tea
Average Price: Modest
Address: 1110 Panatella Boulevard NW
Calgary, AB T3K 0A9
Phone: (403) 269-6088

#211
Savour
Cuisines: Kitchen & Bath, Specialty Food
Average Price: Expensive
Address: 1331 9th Ave SE
Calgary, AB T2G 0T2
Phone: (403) 532-8222

#212
Real Canadian Superstore
Cuisines: Grocery
Average Price: Modest
Address: 20 Heritage Meadows Way SE
Calgary, AB T2H 3C1
Phone: (403) 692-6220

#213
Cookies By George
Cuisines: Desserts
Average Price: Inexpensive
Address: 106-6455 Macleod Trail SW
Calgary, AB T2H 0K8
Phone: (403) 258-4410

#214
Eastgate Restaurant & Lounge
Cuisines: Caterer, Chinese,
Ethnic Food, Nightlife
Average Price: Expensive
Address: 4408 17 Ave SE
Calgary, AB T2A 0T6
Phone: (403) 272-8701

#215
You & I Coffee
Cuisines: Coffee, Tea
Average Price: Inexpensive
Address: 700 4 Ave SW
Calgary, AB T2P 3J4
Phone: (403) 262-6044

#216
Apna Desi Meat Masala
Cuisines: Deli, Sandwiches, Meat Shop
Average Price: Modest
Address: 5075 Falconridge Boulevard NE
Calgary, AB T3J 3K9
Phone: (403) 568-4455

#217
Daltons Steak & Seafood
Cuisines: Seafood, Meat Shop
Average Price: Modest
Address: 3515 26 St NE
Calgary, AB T1Y 7E3
Phone: (403) 291-9225

#218
Waves Coffee House
Cuisines: Coffee, Tea
Average Price: Modest
Address: 30 Springborough Boulevard SW
Calgary, AB T3H 5M6
Phone: (403) 217-0300

#219
3:30 Teatime Bubble
Cuisines: Juice Bar, Coffee, Tea
Average Price: Inexpensive
Address: 108 3 Avenue SW
Calgary, AB T2P 0E7
Phone: (403) 984-2881

#220
Lakeview Bakery
Cuisines: Bakery
Average Price: Expensive
Address: 6449 Crowchild Trail SW
Calgary, AB T3E 5R7
Phone: (403) 246-6127

#221
Gravity Espresso & Wine Bar
Cuisines: Coffee, Tea
Average Price: Modest
Address: 909 10 Street SE
Calgary, AB T2G 0S8
Phone: (403) 457-0697

#222
Baya Rica Cafe
Cuisines: Coffee, Tea
Average Price: Modest
Address: 204 7A St NE
Calgary, AB T2E 4E8
Phone: (403) 261-2618

#223
Say Cheese Fromagerie
Cuisines: Cheese Shop
Average Price: Modest
Address: 1235 26 Avenue SE
Calgary, AB T2G 1R7
Phone: (403) 262-7530

#224
Chocolaterie Bernard Callebaut
Cuisines: Chocolate Shop
Average Price: Expensive
Address: 847 17 Ave SW
Calgary, AB T2T 0A1
Phone: (403) 244-1665

#225
Cinnzeo Bakery & Cafe
Cuisines: Bakery
Average Price: Modest
Address: 3625 Shaganappi Trl NW
Calgary, AB T3A 0E2
Phone: (403) 202-4000

#226
August Moon
Cuisines: Chinese, Ethnic Food
Average Price: Modest
Address: 9630 Elbow Dr SW
Calgary, AB T2V 1M2
Phone: (403) 255-7793

#227
Arirang Oriental Food Store
Cuisines: Ethnic Food, Grocery
Average Price: Modest
Address: 1324 10 Avenue SW
Calgary, AB T3C
Phone: (403) 228-0980

#228
Tim Hortons
Cuisines: Coffee, Tea
Average Price: Inexpensive
Address: 7101 Macleod Trl SW
Calgary, AB T2H 0L8
Phone: (403) 255-4886

#229
Orchid Room Fusion Cuisine
Cuisines: Asian Fusion,
Ethnic Food, Vietnamese
Average Price: Modest
Address: Bankers Hall
Calgary, AB T2P 4K1
Phone: (403) 263-4457

#230
Wilde Grainz
Cuisines: Bakery
Average Price: Modest
Address: 1218C 9 Aveune SE
Calgary, AB T2G 3H8
Phone: (403) 767-9006

#231
Starbucks
Cuisines: Coffee, Tea
Average Price: Modest
Address: 320 4th Ave SW
Calgary, AB T2P 2S6
Phone: (403) 266-1611

#232
Costco Liquor
Cuisines: Beer, Wine, Spirits
Average Price: Modest
Address: 83 Heritage Gate SE
Calgary, AB T2H 3A7
Phone: (403) 252-7129

#233
Kwanzaa Coffee House
Cuisines: Coffee, Tea
Average Price: Modest
Address: 1824 Crowchild Trail Northwest
Calgary, AB T2M 3Y7
Phone: (403) 282-7881

#234
Tim Hortons
Cuisines: Coffee, Tea, Fast Food,
Breakfast & Brunch
Average Price: Inexpensive
Address: 3840 Macleod Trail SE
Calgary, AB T2G 2R2
Phone: (403) 287-7780

#235
**Loriz Pilipino Bakery
& Convenience Store**
Cuisines: Bakery, Ethnic Food,
Convenience Store
Average Price: Inexpensive
Address: 8330 Macleod Trl SE
Calgary, AB T2H 2V2
Phone: (403) 278-8660

#236
Starbucks
Cuisines: Coffee, Tea
Average Price: Modest
Address: 100 Anderson Road SE
Calgary, AB T2J 3V1
Phone: (403) 278-4976

#237
**Khublai Mongolian
Szechuan Cuisine**
Cuisines: Chinese, Mongolian, Ethnic Food
Average Price: Modest
Address: 349 10 Ave SW
Calgary, AB T2R 0A5
Phone: (403) 232-8800

#238
Caffe Francesco
Cuisines: Grocery, Italian, Deli
Average Price: Modest
Address: 3413 26 Avenue SW
Calgary, AB T3E 0N3
Phone: (403) 249-1151

#239
Calgary Co-Op Wines & Spirits
Cuisines: Beer, Wine, Spirits
Average Price: Inexpensive
Address: 336 16 Avenue NW
Calgary, AB T2M 0H6
Phone: (403) 299-4268

#240
Dawsco Coffee Service
Cuisines: Coffee, Tea
Average Price: Inexpensive
Address: 4325 1 Street SE
Calgary, AB T2G 2L2
Phone: (403) 250-7494

#241
Starbucks
Cuisines: Coffee, Tea
Average Price: Modest
Address: 315 8 Ave SW
Calgary, AB T2P 4K1
Phone: (403) 261-0669

#242
Coco Karamel
Cuisines: Desserts
Average Price: Exclusive
Address: 2110-41 Avenue NE
Calgary, AB T2H 0M1
Phone: (403) 990-3634

#243
Dakota Deli
Cuisines: Deli, Sandwiches, Donairs
Average Price: Inexpensive
Address: 706 9 Street SW
Calgary, AB T2P 2B4
Phone: (403) 269-9666

#244
Patisserie Du Soleil
Cuisines: Bakery
Average Price: Modest
Address: 1600 90 Ave SW
Calgary, AB T2V 5A8
Phone: (403) 259-5864

#245
Cobs Bread
Cuisines: Bakery
Average Price: Modest
Address: 150 Crowfoot Crescent NW
Calgary, AB T3G 3T2
Phone: (403) 239-2666

#246
Coffee & S'cream
Cuisines: Coffee, Tea, Ice Cream
Average Price: Inexpensive
Address: 555 Northmount Drive NW
Calgary, AB T2K 3J3
Phone: (403) 210-2020

#247
Master Meats
Cuisines: Meat Shop, Butcher
Average Price: Modest
Address: 120 40 Avenue NW
Calgary, AB T2K 0E3
Phone: (403) 277-5002

#248
Riverbend Peking House
Cuisines: Chinese, Ethnic Food
Average Price: Modest
Address: 8338 18 Street SE
Calgary, AB T2C 4E4
Phone: (403) 279-8134

#249
Orchid Pastry
Cuisines: Desserts
Average Price: Modest
Address: 6219 Centre Street N
Calgary, AB T2K 0V2
Phone: (403) 457-5757

#250
Dairy Queen
Cuisines: Fast Food, Ice Cream
Average Price: Inexpensive
Address: 1919 Southland Dr SW
Calgary, AB T2W 0K1
Phone: (403) 252-7283

#251
Golden West Restaurant
Cuisines: Ethnic Food
Average Price: Inexpensive
Address: 4620A Bowness Rd NW
Calgary, AB T3B 0B3
Phone: (403) 288-6111

#252
CRMR At Home
Cuisines: Specialty Food
Average Price: Expensive
Address: 330 17 Avenue SW
Calgary, AB T2S 0A8
Phone: (403) 532-0241

#253
LP Family Foods
Cuisines: Grocery
Average Price: Modest
Address: 1312 17 Ave SW
Calgary, AB T3C
Phone: (403) 245-9131

#254
Hear's My Soul
Cuisines: Coffee, Tea
Average Price: Modest
Address: 107 535 8th Avenue SE
Calgary, AB T2G 0M4
Phone: (587) 350-2200

#255
Yummi Yogis
Cuisines: Food Truck, Vegetarian
Average Price: Inexpensive
Address: Calgary, AB T2B 1P1
Phone: (403) 472-5655

#256
Bliss & Co. Cupcakes & Desserts
Cuisines: Bakery
Average Price: Modest
Address: 6455 Macleod Trl SW
Calgary, AB T2H 0K8
Phone: (403) 281-8821

#257
Red Tree Catering
Cuisines: Caterer, Bakery, Delicatessen
Average Price: Expensive
Address: 2129 33 Avenue SW
Calgary, AB T2T 1Z7
Phone: (403) 242-3246

#258
Sweetly Speaking
Cuisines: Chocolate Shop
Average Price: Modest
Address: 301 14 Street Nw
Calgary, AB T2N 1Z7
Phone: (403) 891-2755

#259
Starbucks
Cuisines: Coffee, Tea
Average Price: Modest
Address: 9th Ave SE
Calgary, AB T2G 0S7
Phone: (403) 263-0612

#260
Cambrian Pharmacy
Cuisines: Drugstore, Food
Average Price: Exclusive
Address: 728 Northmount Dr NW
Calgary, AB T2K 3K2
Phone: (403) 289-9181

#261
Umi Sushi Express
Cuisines: Food
Average Price: Modest
Address: 2500 University Drive North West
Calgary, AB T1H 1N1
Phone: (403) 202-9233

#262
Blue River Bistro
Cuisines: Coffee, Tea, Delicatessen,
Sandwiches
Average Price: Expensive
Address: 227 11 Ave SW
Calgary, AB T2R 1R9
Phone: (403) 650-2812

#263
The Liquor Depot
Cuisines: Beer, Wine, Spirits
Average Price: Modest
Address: 1140 17 Avenue SW
Calgary, AB T2T 0B4
Phone: (403) 229-2367

#264
Coffee Cats Cafe
Cuisines: Coffee, Tea, Café
Average Price: Modest
Address: 2765 17 Avenue SW
Calgary, AB T3E 7E1
Phone: (403) 240-1842

#265
Leonidas Chocolates
Cuisines: Chocolate Shop
Average Price: Modest
Address: 815 49 Avenue SW
Calgary, AB T2S 1G8
Phone: (403) 287-1717

#266
Booster Juice
Cuisines: Food
Average Price: Modest
Address: 3221 Sunridge Way NE
Calgary, AB T1Y 7M4
Phone: (403) 291-3477

#267
Yogen Fruz
Cuisines: Juice Bar, Ice Cream
Average Price: Modest
Address: 3625 Shanganappi Trl NW
Calgary, AB T3A 0E2
Phone: (403) 286-6686

#268
Planet Organic Market
Cuisines: Shopping, Health Market
Average Price: Expensive
Address: 10233 Elbow Drive SW
Calgary, AB T2W 1E8
Phone: (403) 252-2404

#269
By The Cup Coffee
Cuisines: Food
Average Price: Inexpensive
Address: 736 8 Avenue SW
Calgary, AB T2P 1H4
Phone: (403) 233-2708

#270
Hong Kong Food Market
Cuisines: Grocery
Average Price: Modest
Address: 3215 17 Avenue SE
Calgary, AB T2A 0R1
Phone: (403) 387-7798

#271
Mina's Vietnamese Noodle Soup
Cuisines: Specialty Food
Average Price: Inexpensive
Address: 12100 Macleod Trail SE
Calgary, AB T2J 7G9
Phone: (403) 225-8954

#272
The Cheesecake Company
Cuisines: Desserts, Diner,
Breakfast & Brunch
Average Price: Modest
Address: 5615 Northland Drive NW
Calgary, AB T2L 2J7
Phone: (403) 247-2407

#273
Pies Plus
Cuisines: Bakery, Desserts
Average Price: Inexpensive
Address: 12445 Lake Fraser Dr SE
Calgary, AB T2J 7A4
Phone: (403) 271-6616

#274
Hillhurst Sunnyside Farmer's Market
Cuisines: Farmers Market
Average Price: Modest
Address: 1320 5 Avenue NW
Calgary, AB T2N 0S2
Phone: (403) 283-0554

#275
Tim Hortons
Cuisines: Coffee, Tea, Donuts, Sandwiches
Average Price: Inexpensive
Address: 8338 18 St SE
Calgary, AB T2C 4E4
Phone: (403) 236-0291

#276
Crêpes & Cravings
Cuisines: Crêperie, Ice Cream
Average Price: Inexpensive
Address: 1013 17 Avenue SW
Calgary, AB T2T 1A7
Phone: (403) 228-6523

#277
Real Canadian Superstore
Cuisines: Grocery
Average Price: Modest
Address: 5251 Country Hills Boulevard NW
Calgary, AB T3A 5H8
Phone: (403) 241-4027

#278
Csn Wine & Spirits
Cuisines: Beer, Wine, Spirits
Average Price: Expensive
Address: 1716 Centre Street NE
Calgary, AB T2E 2S4
Phone: (403) 296-0240

#279
Second Cup Kensington
Cuisines: Coffee, Tea
Average Price: Inexpensive
Address: 338 10 Street NW
Calgary, AB T2N 1V8
Phone: (403) 244-4465

#280
A Wish Cake & Café
Cuisines: Bakery
Average Price: Modest
Address: 901 6th Avenue SW
Calgary, AB T2P 3E5
Phone: (403) 699-8839

#281
Popeye's Supplements Calgary
Cuisines: Shopping, Health Market
Average Price: Modest
Address: 3810 Macleod Trl SE
Calgary, AB T2G 2R2
Phone: (403) 287-2226

#282
Oil & Vinegar
Cuisines: Specialty Food
Average Price: Expensive
Address: T154, 317 7th Avenue SW
Calgary, AB T2P 2Y9
Phone: (403) 699-9672

#283
Pizza Master Fusion
Cuisines: Ethnic Food, Pizza
Average Price: Modest
Address: 5 Coral Springs Blvd NE
Calgary, AB T3J 4J1
Phone: (403) 263-3334

#284
Booster Juice
Cuisines: Juice Bar
Average Price: Inexpensive
Address: 314 10 St NW
Calgary, AB T2N 1V8
Phone: (403) 270-2704

#285
Tim Hortons
Cuisines: Coffee, Tea
Average Price: Inexpensive
Address: 5 Heritage Gate SE
Calgary, AB T2H 3A7
Phone: (403) 692-6629

#286
Heart's Choices
Cuisines: Farmers Market
Average Price: Modest
Address: 510 77th Avenue SE
Calgary, AB T2H 1C3
Phone: (403) 889-0993

#287
Watermill Bakery
Cuisines: Bakery
Average Price: Modest
Address: 5403 Crowchild Trail NW
Calgary, AB T3B 4Z1
Phone: (403) 450-4995

#288
Bamboo Gardens
Cuisines: Ethnic Food
Average Price: Modest
Address: 1603 18 St NE
Calgary, AB T2E 4W2
Phone: (403) 277-1246

#289
Starbucks
Cuisines: Coffee, Tea
Average Price: Inexpensive
Address: 1200 37 Street SW
Calgary, AB T3C 1S2
Phone: (403) 217-2485

#290
Thai Manna
Cuisines: Do-It-Yourself Food
Average Price: Expensive
Address: 7711 Macleod Trl SW
Calgary, AB T2H
Phone: (403) 998-7049

#291
Cob's Bread
Cuisines: Bakery
Average Price: Modest
Address: 1941 Uxbridge Drive NW
Calgary, AB T2N 2V2
Phone: (403) 282-1779

#292
Purdy's Chocolates
Cuisines: Chocolate Shop
Average Price: Modest
Address: 3625 Shaganappi Trl NW
Calgary, AB T3A 0E2
Phone: (403) 286-1122

#293
Tea & Collection
Cuisines: Coffee, Tea
Average Price: Expensive
Address: 1623 Centre Street NW
Calgary, AB T2E 8S7
Phone: (403) 276-7778

#294
Ohh La La Patisserie
Cuisines: Bakery
Average Price: Exclusive
Address: 8561 8 A Avenue SW
Calgary, AB T3H 0V5
Phone: (587) 353-0111

#295
Rocky Mountain Chocolate Factory
Cuisines: Chocolate Shop, Candy Store
Average Price: Expensive
Address: 2525 36th St NE
Calgary, AB T1Y 5T4
Phone: (403) 590-4110

#296
Pearl House
Cuisines: Coffee, Tea
Average Price: Inexpensive
Address: 328 Centre Street Southeast
Calgary, AB T2G 4X6
Phone: (403) 264-8888

#297
Safeway Food & Drug
Cuisines: Deli, Sandwiches, Grocery
Average Price: Expensive
Address: 410 10 St NW
Calgary, AB T2N 1V9
Phone: (403) 270-8381

#298
Calgary Coop
Cuisines: Grocery
Average Price: Modest
Address: 4940 Richmond Road SW
Calgary, AB T3E 6K4
Phone: (403) 299-4490

#299
Village Ice Cream
Cuisines: Ice Cream
Average Price: Modest
Address: 431 10 Avenue SE
Calgary, AB T2G 0W3
Phone: (403) 261-7950

#300
Caffe Artigiano
Cuisines: Coffee, Tea
Average Price: Modest
Address: 332 6th Avenue SW
Calgary, AB T2P 0B2
Phone: (403) 699-9855

#301
Jugo Juice-Western Canadian Place
Cuisines: Juice Bar
Average Price: Modest
Address: 801 6 St SW
Calgary, AB T2P 3V8
Phone: (403) 261-9706

#302
Nottinghams Pub & Restaurant
Cuisines: Pub, American, Beer, Wine, Spirits
Average Price: Inexpensive
Address: 8060 Silver Springs Boulevard NW
Calgary, AB T3B 5K1
Phone: (403) 288-0964

#303
Lambda Oriental Foods Supermarket
Cuisines: Ethnic Food, Grocery
Average Price: Modest
Address: 1423 Centre Street Northwest
Calgary, AB T2E 2R8
Phone: (403) 230-1916

#304
Starbucks
Cuisines: Coffee, Tea
Average Price: Modest
Address: 110 9th Ave SE
Calgary, AB T2G 5A6
Phone: (403) 266-7331

#305
The Candy Kid
Cuisines: Candy Store
Average Price: Modest
Address: 225 10th Street NW
Calgary, AB T2N 1V5
Phone: (403) 270-7744

#306
Chocolaterie Bernard Callebaut
Cuisines: Chocolate Shop
Average Price: Expensive
Address: 1123 Kensington Rd NW
Calgary, AB T2N 3P2
Phone: (403) 283-5550

#307
Ryan's Meat Processors
Cuisines: Meat Shop
Average Price: Modest
Address: 1916 30 Avenue NE
Calgary, AB T2E 7B2
Phone: (403) 250-7727

#308
Starbucks
Cuisines: Coffee, Tea
Average Price: Modest
Address: 1200 37 Street SW
Calgary, AB T3C 1S2
Phone: (403) 217-2485

#309
Ruby's Kitchen
Cuisines: Ethnic Food
Average Price: Modest
Address: 3132 26th St. NE
Calgary, AB T1Y 6Z1
Phone: (403) 452-7965

#310
**A Ladybug Organic Foods
& Belgium Bakery**
Cuisines: Bakery
Average Price: Modest
Address: 510 42 Ave SE
Calgary, AB T2G 1Y6
Phone: (403) 287-1137

#311
Mac's Convenience Store
Cuisines: Convenience Store
Average Price: Inexpensive
Address: 705 8 St SW
Calgary, AB T2P 2A8
Phone: (403) 262-3055

#312
Mcgavin's Bread Basket
Cuisines: Bakery
Average Price: Inexpensive
Address: 9250 Macleod Trail SE
Calgary, AB T2J 0P5
Phone: (403) 253-2284

#313
Starbucks
Cuisines: Coffee, Tea
Average Price: Modest
Address: 10816 Macleod Trail SE
Calgary, AB T2J 5N8
Phone: (403) 278-0500

#314
T & T Supermarket
Cuisines: Grocery, Ethnic Food
Average Price: Modest
Address: 3516 8 Avenue NE
Calgary, AB T2A 6K5
Phone: (403) 569-6888

#315
Lucky Supermarket
Cuisines: Grocery
Average Price: Modest
Address: 4527 8 Ave SE
Calgary, AB T2A 0A7
Phone: (403) 569-0778

#316
Monplaisir Delicacies
Cuisines: Chocolate Shop, Candy Store
Average Price: Modest
Address: 751 3rd Street SW
Calgary, AB T2P 4K8
Phone: (587) 538-0690

#317
O Cup
Cuisines: Coffee, Tea
Average Price: Inexpensive
Address: 110 2nd Avenue SE
Calgary, AB T2G 0B3
Phone: (403) 452-2608

#318
Savour Coffee
Cuisines: Coffee, Tea
Average Price: Modest
Address: 2500 4th Street SW
Calgary, AB T2S 1X6
Phone: (587) 353-5370

#319
Rainbow Bakery
Cuisines: Bakery
Average Price: Inexpensive
Address: 328 Centre Street Southeast
Calgary, AB T2G 4X6
Phone: (403) 234-9909

#320
Community Natural Foods
Cuisines: Organic Store, Grocery
Average Price: Expensive
Address: 850 Crowfoot Crescent NW
Calgary, AB T3G 0B4
Phone: (403) 930-6363

#321
Real Canadian Superstore
Cuisines: Grocery
Average Price: Inexpensive
Address: 7020 4th Street NW
Calgary, AB T2K 1C4
Phone: (403) 516-8519

#322
Olivier's Candies
Cuisines: Candy Store, Chocolate Shop
Average Price: Modest
Address: 1316 9 Ave SE
Calgary, AB T2G 0T3
Phone: (403) 275-5195

#323
Rise Bakery
Cuisines: Coffee, Tea, Bakery
Average Price: Modest
Address: Penn West Plaza
Calgary, AB T2P 1K3
Phone: (403) 265-7765

#324
Starbucks
Cuisines: Coffee, Tea
Average Price: Modest
Address: 11566 24 Street SE
Calgary, AB T2Z 3J3
Phone: (403) 236-4531

#325
Cococo Cafe
Cuisines: Chocolate Shop
Average Price: Modest
Address: 339 Aspen Glen Landing SW
Calgary, AB T3H 4A3
Phone: (403) 265-1019

#326
City Fish
Cuisines: Seafood Market
Average Price: Modest
Address: 3515 27 Street NE
Calgary, AB T1Y 5E4
Phone: (403) 250-8222

#327
Starbucks
Cuisines: Coffee, Tea
Average Price: Expensive
Address: 400 3 Avenue SW
Calgary, AB T2P 4H2
Phone: (403) 532-9375

#328
St Laurent Cake House
Cuisines: Bakery
Average Price: Inexpensive
Address: 303 Centre Street SW
Calgary, AB T2G 2B9
Phone: (403) 262-1168

#329
Starbucks
Cuisines: Coffee, Tea
Average Price: Modest
Address: 450 1 St SW
Calgary, AB T2P 5H1
Phone: (403) 262-8200

#330
T & T Supermarket
Cuisines: Grocery
Average Price: Modest
Address: 9650 Harvest Hills Boulevard NE
Calgary, AB T3K 0B3
Phone: (403) 237-6608

#331
Saigon Red Sky
Cuisines: Ethnic Food, Vietnamese
Average Price: Inexpensive
Address: 176 Bedford Drive NE
Calgary, AB T3K 1K2
Phone: (403) 265-8668

#332
100 Tops Supermarket
Cuisines: Grocery
Average Price: Modest
Address: 1623 Centre St NW
Calgary, AB T2E 8S7
Phone: (403) 276-8889

#333
Urban Bean Coffee Company
Cuisines: Coffee, Tea
Average Price: Modest
Address: 702 7 Ave SW
Calgary, AB T2P 0Z1
Phone: (403) 264-8630

#334
Oak & Vine
Cuisines: Beer, Wine, Spirits
Average Price: Modest
Address: 1030 16th Ave NW
Calgary, AB T2M 0K5
Phone: (403) 453-2294

#335
Caffè Artigiano
Cuisines: Coffee, Tea
Average Price: Modest
Address: 400 4th St SW
Calgary, AB T2P 2H5
Phone: (403) 262-2343

#336
Starbucks
Cuisines: Coffee, Tea
Average Price: Modest
Address: 255 5 Avenue SW
Calgary, AB T2P 3G6
Phone: (403) 237-0670

#337
Safeway Food & Drug
Cuisines: Deli, Grocery, Bakery
Average Price: Modest
Address: 524 Elbow Dr SW
Calgary, AB T2S 2H6
Phone: (403) 228-3520

#338
Sweet Surprise
Cuisines: Candy Store
Average Price: Modest
Address: 200 Barclay Parade SW
Calgary, AB T2P 4R5
Phone: (403) 777-1881

#339
Good Earth Cafe
Cuisines: Coffee, Tea
Average Price: Modest
Address: 1600 90th Avenue SW
Calgary, AB T2V 5A8
Phone: (403) 212-1224

#340
Starbucks
Cuisines: Coffee, Tea
Average Price: Modest
Address: 919 Centre Street NW
Calgary, AB T2E 2P6
Phone: (403) 230-7844

#341
Extreme Bean
Cuisines: Coffee, Tea
Average Price: Modest
Address: 3303 3 Ave NW
Calgary, AB T2N 0M1
Phone: (403) 283-6820

#342
Mac's Convenience Stores
Cuisines: Convenience Store
Average Price: Inexpensive
Address: 555 11 Ave SW
Calgary, AB T2R 1P6
Phone: (403) 266-6585

#343
Concept
Cuisines: Beer, Wine, Spirits
Average Price: Modest
Address: 908 17 Ave SW
Calgary, AB T2T 0A2
Phone: (403) 228-1006

#344
Symon's Valley Ranch
Cuisines: Farmers Market
Average Price: Modest
Address: 14555 Symons Valley Road NW
Calgary, AB T3R 1J1
Phone: (403) 774-7246

#345
Second Cup
Cuisines: Coffee, Tea, Juice Bar
Average Price: Modest
Address: 607 8th Ave SW
Calgary, AB T2P 0A7
Phone: (403) 237-9172

#346
Mac's Convenience Store
Cuisines: Convenience Store
Average Price: Inexpensive
Address: 528 4th Ave SW
Calgary, AB T2P
Phone: (403) 264-7391

#347
Citadel Cafe
Cuisines: Food
Average Price: Inexpensive
Address: 240 4 Avenue SW
Calgary, AB T2P 4H4
Phone: (403) 265-0488

#348
Jing Jing Bakery
Cuisines: Bakery
Average Price: Inexpensive
Address: 100 3rd Avenue S.E.
Calgary, AB T2G 0B6
Phone: (403) 265-9588

#349
Good Earth Cafe
Cuisines: Coffee, Tea
Average Price: Modest
Address: 200 Barclay Parade SW
Calgary, AB T2P 4R5
Phone: (403) 237-8684

#350
Minhas Micro Brewery
Cuisines: Brewerie
Average Price: Modest
Address: 1314 44 Avenue NE
Calgary, AB T2E 6L6
Phone: (403) 695-3701

#351
Big Rock Brewery
Cuisines: Brewerie
Average Price: Modest
Address: 5555 76 Ave SE
Calgary, AB T2C 4L8
Phone: (403) 720-3239

#352
A Ladybug Bakery And Cafe
Cuisines: Bakery, Desserts
Average Price: Expensive
Address: 2132 10 Aspen Stone Blvd
Calgary, AB T3H 5Z2
Phone: (403) 249-5530

#353
Fresh Kitchen
Cuisines: Food
Average Price: Expensive
Address: 2042 - 42 Ave SW
Calgary, AB T2T 2M7
Phone: (403) 214-7771

#354
Fruiticana
Cuisines: Fruits, Veggies,
Ethnic Food, Grocery
Average Price: Inexpensive
Address: 5075 Falconridge Blvd NE
Calgary, AB T3J 3K9
Phone: (403) 590-1611

#355
Real Canadian Superstore
Cuisines: Grocery
Average Price: Inexpensive
Address: 5858 Signal Hill Centre SW
Calgary, AB T3H
Phone: (403) 686-8036

#356
The Wine Shop
Cuisines: Beer, Wine, Spirits
Average Price: Modest
Address: 856 16 Ave SW
Calgary, AB T2S 0B7
Phone: (403) 228-4320

#357
Starbucks
Cuisines: Coffee, Tea
Average Price: Modest
Address: 7616 Elbow Dr SW
Calgary, AB T2V 1K2
Phone: (403) 253-4602

#358
Cobs Bread
Cuisines: Bakery
Average Price: Inexpensive
Address: 500 Country Hills Blvd NE
Calgary, AB T3K 4Y7
Phone: (403) 226-5555

#359
Chocolaterie Bernard Callebaut
Cuisines: Chocolate Shop
Average Price: Modest
Address: 6455 Macleod Trail South
Calgary, AB T2H 0K8
Phone: (403) 252-5334

#360
Sunnyside Natural Market
Cuisines: Health Market, Grocery
Average Price: Modest
Address: 338 10 St NW
Calgary, AB T2N 1V8
Phone: (403) 270-7477

#361
Cobs Bread
Cuisines: Bakery
Average Price: Expensive
Address: 10801 Bonaventure Drive SE
Calgary, AB T2J 6Z8
Phone: (403) 278-6988

#362
Bin 905 Wine & Spirits
Cuisines: Beer, Wine, Spirits
Average Price: Expensive
Address: 2311 4th St SW
Calgary, AB T2S 0K3
Phone: (403) 261-1600

#363
Luubaan Restaurant
Cuisines: Ethnic Food
Average Price: Modest
Address: 1506 12 Ave SW
Calgary, AB T3C 0R2
Phone: (403) 452-2452

#364
Quickly Premium Bubble Tea
Cuisines: Coffee, Tea
Average Price: Inexpensive
Address: 110 2nd Avenue SE
Calgary, AB T2G
Phone: (403) 719-6084

#365
Treasures Of China
Cuisines: Chinese, Ethnic Food
Average Price: Modest
Address: 9125 Bonaventure Dr SE
Calgary, AB T2J 0P9
Phone: (403) 252-6888

#366
Kay's Food Market
Cuisines: Grocery
Average Price: Modest
Address: 935 6 Ave SW
Calgary, AB T2P 0V7
Phone: (403) 261-5655

#367
Amaranth 4th Street Market
Cuisines: Organic Store, Grocery
Average Price: Expensive
Address: 1407 4th Street SW
Calgary, AB T2R 0Y1
Phone: (403) 457-3663

#368
The Home Vintner
Cuisines: Winery
Average Price: Modest
Address: 4404 14 Street NW
Calgary, AB T2K 1J5
Phone: (403) 284-0486

#369
A Cookie Occasion
Cuisines: Desserts
Average Price: Inexpensive
Address: 2107 33 Ave SW
Calgary, AB T2T 1Z7
Phone: (403) 246-6700

#370
Hunterhorn Bakery
Cuisines: Bakery
Average Price: Inexpensive
Address: 6692 4th Street N.E.
Calgary, AB T2K 6H1
Phone: (403) 295-1050

#371
Silver Sage Beef
Cuisines: Butcher, Farmers Market
Average Price: Modest
Address: 510 77th Avenue SE
Calgary, AB T2H 1C3
Phone: (403) 804-2184

#372
Tim Hortons
Cuisines: Food
Average Price: Inexpensive
Address: 2000 Airport Road NE
Calgary, AB T2E 6W5
Phone: (403) 221-1786

#373
Amaranth Whole Foods Market
Cuisines: Health Market, Grocery
Average Price: Expensive
Address: 7 Arbour Lake Drive NW
Calgary, AB T3G 5G8
Phone: (403) 547-6333

#374
Mythic Cafe
Cuisines: Food
Average Price: Expensive
Address: 8180 Macleod Trail SE
Calgary, AB T2H 2B8
Phone: (403) 253-2060

#375
Chocolaterie Bernard Callebaut
Cuisines: Chocolate Shop
Average Price: Expensive
Address: 100 Anderson Rd SE
Calgary, AB T2J 3V1
Phone: (403) 271-4100

#376
Cut-Rite Meats
Cuisines: Meat Shop
Average Price: Inexpensive
Address: 2424 50 Street SE
Calgary, AB T2B 1M7
Phone: (403) 272-5159

#377
Sichani's Mediterranean
Cuisines: Farmers Market
Average Price: Inexpensive
Address: 7711 Macleod Trail S
Calgary, AB T2H 0M1
Phone: (403) 607-3714

#378
Bulk Barn
Cuisines: Do-It-Yourself Food,
Herbs & Spices
Average Price: Inexpensive
Address: 9250 Mcleod Trail SE
Calgary, AB T2J 0P5
Phone: (403) 252-5232

#379
Good Earth Cafe
Cuisines: Coffee, Tea
Average Price: Inexpensive
Address: 908 13th Ave SW
Calgary, AB T2R 1A4
Phone: (403) 455-6255

#380
Los Chilitos
Cuisines: Farmers Market, Mexican
Average Price: Modest
Address: 510 77th Ave SE
Calgary, AB T2H 1C3
Phone: (403) 240-9113

#381
Tim Hortons
Cuisines: Food
Average Price: Inexpensive
Address: 2021 Pegasus Road NE
Calgary, AB T2E 8C3
Phone: (403) 250-3395

#382
The Coffee Company
Cuisines: Coffee, Tea
Average Price: Inexpensive
Address: 2500 University Drive N.W
Calgary, AB T2N 1N4
Phone: (403) 289-4947

#383
Sprague Drug
Cuisines: Drugstore, Convenience Store
Average Price: Modest
Address: 727 7 Ave SW
Calgary, AB T2P 0Z5
Phone: (403) 264-7195

#384
Second Cup
Cuisines: Coffee, Tea
Average Price: Expensive
Address: 3625 Shaganappi Trail NW
Calgary, AB T3A 0E2
Phone: (403) 286-2060

#385
Tim Hortons
Cuisines: Donuts, Coffee, Tea, Bagels
Average Price: Inexpensive
Address: 4015 Centre St NW
Calgary, AB T2E 2Y4
Phone: (403) 230-8999

#386
Willow Park Wines & Spirits
Cuisines: Beer, Wine, Spirits
Average Price: Expensive
Address: 4012 Bow Trl SW
Calgary, AB T2E 4Y7
Phone: (403) 777-1234

#387
Davidstea
Cuisines: Coffee, Tea, Tea Room
Average Price: Modest
Address: 843 17th Avenue SW
Calgary, AB T2S 0B7
Phone: (403) 245-3794

#388
5 Vines Wine, Craft Beer & Spirits
Cuisines: Beer, Wine, Spirits
Average Price: Modest
Address: 218 12 Avenue SE
Calgary, AB T2G
Phone: (587) 955-9221

#389
Zyn
Cuisines: Beer, Wine, Spirits
Average Price: Modest
Address: 111 Fifth Avenue SW
Calgary, AB T2P 3G6
Phone: (403) 863-8970

#390
Second Cup
Cuisines: Coffee, Tea
Average Price: Modest
Address: 2803 17 Avenue SW
Calgary, AB T3E 0A8
Phone: (403) 240-1502

#391
Vine Styles
Cuisines: Beer, Wine, Spirits
Average Price: Modest
Address: 833 10th Avenue SW
Calgary, AB T2R 0B4
Phone: (403) 474-5955

#392
Kernels Extraordinary Popcorn
Cuisines: Specialty Food
Average Price: Inexpensive
Address: 3625 Shaganappi Trl NW
Calgary, AB T3A 0E2
Phone: (403) 286-6167

#393
The Liquor Depot
Cuisines: Beer, Wine, Spirits
Average Price: Modest
Address: 3630 Brentwood Rd NW
Calgary, AB T2L 1K8
Phone: (403) 289-2946

#394
Manila Convenience Store
Cuisines: Convenience Store
Average Price: Inexpensive
Address: 10325 Bonaventure Drive SE
Calgary, AB T2J 7E4
Phone: (403) 271-1881

#395
Marble Slab Creamery
Cuisines: Ice Cream
Average Price: Modest
Address: 338 Aspen Glen Landing SW
Calgary, AB T3H 0N5
Phone: (403) 685-1944

#396
Kona On The Corner Cafe
Cuisines: Coffee, Tea
Average Price: Modest
Address: 777 10 St SW
Calgary, AB T2P 0W2
Phone: (403) 699-8882

#397
Calgary Co-Op
Cuisines: Gas & Service Station,
Convenience Store
Average Price: Modest
Address: 16 Avenue NE
Calgary, AB T2E 1K4
Phone: (403) 299-4276

#398
Angel's Cappuccino & Ice Cream Bar
Cuisines: Coffee, Tea, Ice Cream
Average Price: Modest
Address: 4105 Montgomery View
Calgary, AB T3B
Phone: (403) 288-8612

#399
Filipino Market
Cuisines: Grocery
Average Price: Inexpensive
Address: 12-3803 26 Ave SW
Calgary, AB T3E 0N8
Phone: (403) 984-8100

#400
Second Cup
Cuisines: Coffee, Tea
Average Price: Modest
Address: 2025 16 Avenue NW
Calgary, AB T2M 0M3
Phone: (403) 282-6778

#401
Wasim's Donair & Pizza
Cuisines: Pizza, Donairs
Average Price: Modest
Address: 2220 68 Street NE
Calgary, AB T1Y 6Y7
Phone: (403) 280-0241

#402
Zyn
Cuisines: Beer, Wine, Spirits
Average Price: Modest
Address: 145-315 8 Avenue SW
Calgary, AB T2P 4K1
Phone: (403) 266-3517

#403
Yogen Fruz
Cuisines: Ice Cream
Average Price: Modest
Address: 245-150 6 Ave SW
Calgary, AB T2P 3Y6
Phone: (403) 770-3025

#404
Good Earth Cafes
Cuisines: Coffee, Tea
Average Price: Inexpensive
Address: 151 Crowfoot Ter NW
Calgary, AB T3G 4J8
Phone: (403) 239-6641

#405
Kim Chee House
Cuisines: Ethnic Food
Average Price: Inexpensive
Address: 303 Centre St SW
Calgary, AB T2G 2B9
Phone: (403) 265-8098

#406
Safeway Mission
Cuisines: Grocery
Average Price: Modest
Address: 524 Elbow Dr SW
Calgary, AB T2S 2H6
Phone: (403) 228-6141

#407
Crave Cookies & Cupcakes
Cuisines: Bakery, Desserts
Average Price: Modest
Address: 1107 Kensington Road NW
Calgary, AB T2N 3P2
Phone: (403) 270-2728

#408
Maxima Bakery & Cake House
Cuisines: Bakery, Desserts
Average Price: Inexpensive
Address: 1423 Centre Street NW
Calgary, AB T2E 2R8
Phone: (403) 277-8988

#409
Cru Juice
Cuisines: Juice Bar
Average Price: Modest
Address: 236 4th Street NE
Calgary, AB T2E 3S2
Phone: (403) 452-5444

#410
Safeway
Cuisines: Grocery
Average Price: Modest
Address: 11011 Bonaventure Dr SE
Calgary, AB T2J 6S1
Phone: (403) 278-5228

#411
Starbucks
Cuisines: Coffee, Tea
Average Price: Modest
Address: 951 General Ave NE
Calgary, AB T2E 9E1
Phone: (403) 269-2006

#412
Fortune Food Product
Cuisines: Ethnic Food
Average Price: Inexpensive
Address: 2404 Centre Street NE
Calgary, AB T2E 2T9
Phone: (403) 276-3686

#413
Starbucks
Cuisines: Coffee, Tea
Average Price: Modest
Address: 3434 25 Street NE
Calgary, AB T1Y 6C1
Phone: (403) 291-2227

#414
Chocolaterie Bernard Callebaut
Cuisines: Chocolate Shop
Average Price: Modest
Address: 1313 1st Street SE
Calgary, AB T2G 5L1
Phone: (403) 265-5777

#415
Jugo Juice
Cuisines: Sandwiches, Juice Bar
Average Price: Modest
Address: 107-163 Quarry Park Boulevard SE
Calgary, AB T2C 4J2
Phone: (403) 203-1036

#416
Save-On-Foods
Cuisines: Grocery, Drugstore
Average Price: Modest
Address: 225 Pantella Hill NW
Calgary, AB T3K
Phone: (403) 384-9780

#417
Yummy Russia
Cuisines: Delicatessen, Grocery
Average Price: Modest
Address: 7515 Macleod Trail
Calgary, AB T2H 0L8
Phone: (403) 719-4607

#418
Starbucks
Cuisines: Coffee, Tea
Average Price: Modest
Address: 1210 8 St SW
Calgary, AB T2R 1L3
Phone: (403) 228-3372

#419
Springbank Cheese Company
Cuisines: Shopping Center, Cheese Shop
Average Price: Expensive
Address: 10816 Macleod Trail SE
Calgary, AB T2J 5N8
Phone: (403) 225-6040

#420
Jugo Juice
Cuisines: Juice Bar
Average Price: Modest
Address: 1154 Kensington Crescent NW
Calgary, AB T2N 1X6
Phone: (403) 270-0120

#421
Purdy's Chocolates
Cuisines: Ice Cream, Chocolate Shop
Average Price: Modest
Address: 3 Street SW
Calgary, AB T2P 0B2
Phone: (403) 237-8717

#422
Bk Liquor
Cuisines: Beer, Wine, Spirits
Average Price: Modest
Address: 833 1 Ave NE
Calgary, AB T2E 0C2
Phone: (403) 237-7746

#423
E-Mart
Cuisines: Grocery
Average Price: Modest
Address: 3702 17 Avenue SW
Calgary, AB T3E 0C2
Phone: (403) 210-5577

#424
Starbucks
Cuisines: Coffee, Tea
Average Price: Modest
Address: 1120 16 Ave NW
Calgary, AB T2M 0K8
Phone: (403) 338-1343

#425
Blush Lane Organic Market
Cuisines: Health Market, Grocery
Average Price: Expensive
Address: 3000 10 Aspen Stone Blvd SW
Calgary, AB T3H 0K3
Phone: (403) 210-1247

#426
Dave's Liquor Store Ltd
Cuisines: Beer, Wine, Spirits
Average Price: Modest
Address: 1546 16 Ave NW
Calgary, AB T2M 0L5
Phone: (403) 220-9483

#427
Cobs Bread
Cuisines: Bakery
Average Price: Inexpensive
Address: 236 Stewart Green SW
Calgary, AB T3H 3C8
Phone: (403) 217-1553

#428
Liquor Box
Cuisines: Beer, Wine, Spirits
Average Price: Modest
Address: 2112 Crowchild Trail Northwest
Calgary, AB T2M 3Y7
Phone: (403) 338-1268

#429
Booster Juice
Cuisines: Juice Bar
Average Price: Inexpensive
Address: 3542 Garrison Gate SW
Calgary, AB T2T 6N1
Phone: (403) 240-3289

#430
Starbucks
Cuisines: Coffee, Tea
Average Price: Inexpensive
Address: 4825 Mount Royal Gate SW
Calgary, AB T3E 7N9
Phone: (403) 440-6328

#431
Sobeys
Cuisines: Grocery
Average Price: Modest
Address: 8338 18 Street SE
Calgary, AB T2C 4E4
Phone: (403) 279-9070

#432
Bamboo-House Chinese Food
Cuisines: Chinese, Ethnic Food
Average Price: Modest
Address: 3304 64 Street NE
Calgary, AB T1Y 5R4
Phone: (403) 285-5455

#433
Cookies On The Go
Cuisines: Bakery, Coffee, Tea
Average Price: Modest
Address: 1935-32 Avenue NE
Calgary, AB T2E 7C8
Phone: (403) 769-9011

#434
Gordons Home Made Sausages
Cuisines: Butcher, Street Vendor
Average Price: Inexpensive
Address: 314 Stepen Avenue
Calgary, AB T2P 4K1
Phone: (403) 288-3007

#435
Jugo Juice
Cuisines: Juice Bar
Average Price: Modest
Address: 2015 4 St SW
Calgary, AB T2S 1W6
Phone: (403) 209-2455

#436
El-Mundo Cafe Bistro
Cuisines: French, Coffee, Tea
Average Price: Inexpensive
Address: 7150 Saint-Hubert Rue
Montreal, QC H2R 2N1
Phone: (514) 272-5553

#437
Join US Convenience Store
Cuisines: Convenience Store
Average Price: Inexpensive
Address: 1039 17 Ave SW
Calgary, AB T2T 0A9
Phone: (403) 244-5503

#438
Fiasco Gelato
Cuisines: Food Truck
Average Price: Modest
Address: 416 Meridian Rd SE A20
Calgary, AB T2A 1X2
Phone: (403) 351-1331

#439
Choklat
Cuisines: Specialty Food
Average Price: Modest
Address: Heritage Drive SE
Calgary, AB
Phone: (403) 457-1419

#440
Marble Slab Creamery
Cuisines: Ice Cream
Average Price: Inexpensive
Address: 6455 Macleod Trail SW
Calgary, AB T2H 0K9
Phone: (403) 301-4140

#441
Merlo Vinoteca
Cuisines: Beer, Wine, Spirits
Average Price: Modest
Address: 10 Aspen Stone Blvd SW
Calgary, AB T3H 0K3
Phone: (403) 269-1338

#442
Starbucks
Cuisines: Coffee, Tea
Average Price: Modest
Address: 1122 Kensington Rd NW
Calgary, AB T2N 3P3
Phone: (403) 521-5217

#443
Solo Liquor Store
Cuisines: Beer, Wine, Spirits
Average Price: Inexpensive
Address: 2141 18 Ave NE
Calgary, AB T2E 1R7
Phone: (403) 250-6600

#444
Jim Hortons
Cuisines: Donairs, Internet Café, Bagels
Average Price: Modest
Address: 815 36th Street NE
Calgary, AB T2A 4W3
Phone: (403) 273-7755

#445
Teaopia Ltd
Cuisines: Coffee, Tea
Average Price: Modest
Address: 515 Marlborough Way NE
Calgary, AB T2A 3C1
Phone: (403) 444-9273

#446
Starbucks
Cuisines: Coffee, Tea
Average Price: Modest
Address: 5570 Signal Hill Center So
Calgary, AB T3H 3P8
Phone: (403) 685-6904

#447
Sunterra Market
Cuisines: Grocery
Average Price: Modest
Address: 22 Aerial Place NE
Calgary, AB T2E
Phone: (403) 261-6772

#448
**Friends Cappuccino Bar
& Bake Shop**
Cuisines: Coffee, Tea
Average Price: Modest
Address: 45 Edenwold Drive NW
Calgary, AB T3A 3S8
Phone: (403) 241-5526

#449
Sili Burgers
Cuisines: Food
Average Price: Modest
Address: 1311 163 Quarry Park
Boulevard SE Calgary, AB T2C 5E3
Phone: (587) 350-3663

#450
Smart Mart
Cuisines: Gas & Service Station,
Convenience Store
Average Price: Inexpensive
Address: 3101 34 Ave SE
Calgary, AB T2B 2M6
Phone: (403) 235-3110

#451
7-Eleven Food Stores
Cuisines: Grocery
Average Price: Inexpensive
Address: 675 Acadia Dr SE
Calgary, AB T2J 2Y1
Phone: (403) 278-2832

#452
Jugo Juice
Cuisines: Sandwiches, Fast Food, Juice Bar
Average Price: Inexpensive
Address: 15 Sunpark Plaza SE
Calgary, AB T2X 3T2
Phone: (403) 254-5170

#453
Caffe Beano
Cuisines: Coffee, Tea
Average Price: Modest
Address: 1613 9 Street SW
Calgary, AB T2T
Phone: (403) 229-1232

#454
Rise Bakery
Cuisines: Bakery, Coffee, Tea
Average Price: Modest
Address: 250 6th Ave SW
Calgary, AB T2P
Phone: (403) 265-7765

#455
Prairie Farms Ab
Cuisines: Grocery
Average Price: Inexpensive
Address: 4421 Quesnay Wood Dr SW
Calgary, AB T3E 7K4
Phone: (403) 242-0402

#456
Tutti Frutti
Cuisines: Ice Cream
Average Price: Inexpensive
Address: 406-500 Country Hills Boulevard
Calgary, AB T3K 5Y9
Phone: (587) 230-8881

#457
Richmond Hill Wines
Cuisines: Beer, Wine, Spirits
Average Price: Expensive
Address: 3715 51 St SW
Calgary, AB T3E 6V2
Phone: (403) 686-1980

#458
Teavana
Cuisines: Coffee, Tea
Average Price: Exclusive
Address: 6455 Macleod Trail
Calgary, AB T2H 0K8
Phone: (403) 251-0021

#459
Tim Hortons
Cuisines: Coffee, Tea, Donuts
Average Price: Inexpensive
Address: 1820 Uxbridge Drive NW
Calgary, AB T2N 3Z1
Phone: (403) 284-0349

#460
Starbucks
Cuisines: Coffee, Tea
Average Price: Modest
Address: 33 Heritage Meadows Way SE
Calgary, AB T2H 3B8
Phone: (403) 253-4518

#461
Fuel For Gold
Cuisines: Coffee, Tea
Average Price: Inexpensive
Address: 2500 University Drive NW
Calgary, AB T2N 1N4
Phone: (403) 210-6200

#462
Basha Foods International
Cuisines: Grocery
Average Price: Modest
Address: 2717 Sunridge Way NE
Calgary, AB T1Y 7K7
Phone: (403) 280-6797

#463
Starbucks
Cuisines: Coffee, Tea
Average Price: Modest
Address: 2525 36 St NE
Calgary, AB T1Y 5T4
Phone: (403) 233-7103

#464
Marble Slab Creamery
Cuisines: Ice Cream
Average Price: Expensive
Address: 3625 Shaganappi Trl NW
Calgary, AB T3A 0E2
Phone: (403) 451-8116

#465
Starbucks
Cuisines: Coffee, Tea
Average Price: Modest
Address: 2000 Airport Rd NE
Calgary, AB T2E 6W5
Phone: (403) 503-2200

#466
Cakeworks
Cuisines: Bakery
Average Price: Expensive
Address: 3132 26 Street NE
Calgary, AB T1Y 6Z1
Phone: (403) 571-2253

#467
Nellie's On 90th
Cuisines: Food
Average Price: Modest
Address: 209-2515 90 Ave SW
Calgary, AB T2V 0L8
Phone: (403) 251-5578

#468
Calgary Co-Op
Cuisines: Grocery, Pharmacy
Average Price: Modest
Address: 410-163 Quarry Park Blvd SE
Calgary, AB T2C 4J2
Phone: (403) 203-4825

#469
Golden Happiness Bakery
Cuisines: Bakery
Average Price: Inexpensive
Address: 4815 35B Street SE
Calgary, AB T2B 3M9
Phone: (403) 207-3383

#470
Good Fortune Vegetarian House
Cuisines: Ethnic Food
Average Price: Inexpensive
Address: 3 Avenue SE
Calgary, AB T2G 4Z4
Phone: (403) 265-2838

#471
Eclair De Lune
Cuisines: Bakery
Average Price: Modest
Address: 510 77th Avenue SE
Calgary, AB T2H 1C3
Phone: (403) 398-8803

#472
Popeye's Supplements Calgary
Cuisines: Health Market
Average Price: Modest
Address: 2020 32 Ave NE
Calgary, AB T2E 6T4
Phone: (403) 269-7722

#473
Yum Bakery
Cuisines: Bakery
Average Price: Modest
Address: 510 77th Ave SE
Calgary, AB T2H 1C3
Phone: (403) 472-1296

#474
Candylicious
Cuisines: Candy Store
Average Price: Expensive
Address: 4829 Macleod Trl SW
Calgary, AB T2G 5C1
Phone: (403) 243-4575

#475
Sobey's
Cuisines: Grocery
Average Price: Expensive
Address: 5105 17 Avenue SE
Calgary, AB T2A 0V8
Phone: (403) 273-9339

#476
Real Canadian Superstore
Cuisines: Department Store, Grocery
Average Price: Modest
Address: 10505 Southport Road SW
Calgary, AB T2J 4L3
Phone: (403) 225-6223

#477
Calgary Co-op Dalhousie
Cuisines: Grocery, Bakery
Average Price: Modest
Address: 5505 Shaganappi Trail NW
Calgary, AB T3A 2C3
Phone: (403) 299-4333

#478
Second Cup Braeside
Cuisines: Coffee, Tea
Average Price: Modest
Address: 1919 Southland Drive SW
Calgary, AB T2W 0K1
Phone: (403) 259-4771

#479
Starbucks
Cuisines: Coffee, Tea
Average Price: Modest
Address: 321 6th Avenue SW
Calgary, AB T2P 3H3
Phone: (403) 234-9035

#480
Ballys Bar & Grill
Cuisines: Pub, Beer, Wine, Spirits
Average Price: Modest
Address: 2905 14 Street SW
Calgary, AB T2T 3V5
Phone: (403) 245-0500

#481
Calgary Co-operative Association
Cuisines: Grocery
Average Price: Modest
Address: 2580 Southland Dr SW
Calgary, AB T2V
Phone: (403) 299-4355

#482
Pho Phu Huong
Cuisines: Food
Average Price: Inexpensive
Address: 55 Castleridge Boulevard
North East Calgary, AB T3J 3J8
Phone: (403) 285-7830

#483
Real Canadian Superstore
Cuisines: Grocery, Department Store
Average Price: Inexpensive
Address: 3575 20th Ave NE
Calgary, AB T1Y 6R3
Phone: (403) 280-8207

#484
Dalbrent Spice Rack
Cuisines: Grocery, Ethnic Food
Average Price: Modest
Address: 3604 52 Ave NW
Calgary, AB T2L 1V9
Phone: (403) 289-1409

#485
Tim Hortons
Cuisines: Food
Average Price: Inexpensive
Address: 575 36 Street NE
Calgary, AB T2A 6K3
Phone: (403) 248-7904

#486
Second Cup
Cuisines: Coffee, Tea
Average Price: Inexpensive
Address: 6455 Macleod Trl SW
Calgary, AB T2H 0K9
Phone: (403) 640-2966

#487
K Liquor Store
Cuisines: Beer, Wine, Spirits
Average Price: Inexpensive
Address: 839 6 Avenue SW
Calgary, AB T2P 0V3
Phone: (403) 269-6407

#488
Starbucks
Cuisines: Coffee, Tea
Average Price: Inexpensive
Address: 723 17 Avenue SW
Calgary, AB T2S 0B6
Phone: (403) 209-2888

#489
Safeway Food & Drug
Cuisines: Grocery, Drugstore
Average Price: Modest
Address: 8120 Beddington Boulevard NW
Calgary, AB T3K 2A8
Phone: (403) 275-7741

#490
Tim Hortons
Cuisines: Food
Average Price: Inexpensive
Address: 401 9 Avenue SW
Calgary, AB T2P 3C5
Phone: (403) 265-9045

#491
Calgary Co-op Liqour Store
Cuisines: Beer, Wine, Spirits
Average Price: Modest
Address: 1110 11th Avenue SW
Calgary, AB T2R 1G2
Phone: (403) 299-4233

#492
Bowness Health Food
Cuisines: Shopping, Health Market
Average Price: Modest
Address: 6435 Bowness Rd NW
Calgary, AB T3B 0E6
Phone: (403) 286-2224

#493
Island Foods
Cuisines: Grocery
Average Price: Modest
Address: 200 Barclay Parade SW
Calgary, AB T2P 4R5
Phone: (403) 262-4380

#494
M & M Meat Shops
Cuisines: Butcher
Average Price: Modest
Address: 2601 14 Street SW
Calgary, AB T2T 3T9
Phone: (403) 244-3776

#495
Canada Safeway
Cuisines: Florist, Grocery, Cards
Average Price: Modest
Address: 1632 14 Avenue NW
Calgary, AB T2N 1M7
Phone: (403) 210-0002

#496
Heritage Bakery & Deli
Cuisines: Deli, Bakery
Average Price: Modest
Address: 1912 37 St SW
Calgary, AB T3E 3A3
Phone: (403) 686-6835

#497
Simple Simon Pies
Cuisines: Desserts
Average Price: Inexpensive
Address: 1235 26 Avenue SE
Calgary, AB T2G 1R7
Phone: (403) 205-3475

#498
Calgary Co-Op
Cuisines: Grocery
Average Price: Modest
Address: 4122 Brentwood Road NW
Calgary, AB T2E 4Y7
Phone: (403) 299-4311

#499
Hi-Ball Restaurant
Cuisines: Chinese, Shopping Center
Average Price: Modest
Address: 1941 Uxbridge Dr NW
Calgary, AB T2N 2V2
Phone: (403) 284-3324

#500
Molson Brewhouse
Cuisines: Brewerie
Average Price: Modest
Address: 2000 Airport Dr NE
Calgary, AB T2E 6W5
Phone: (403) 291-6103

Printed in Great Britain
by Amazon